A Treasury of Australian Painting

PLATE 1   Walter Withers *Tranquil Winter* (1895)

A Treasury of Australian Painting

WILLIAM SPLATT & BARBARA BURTON

Lloyd O'Neil

All the paintings in this book are reproduced by permission of the owners, whose assistance at all stages of production is gratefully acknowledged.

The full title of the painting, the artist and the date of the work are listed adjoining the plates: complete caption details of each work are set out on page 65.

Measurements of paintings are given in centimetres and have been adjusted to the nearest half-centimetre. The titles of paintings follow the form currently used by their owners.

A list of public collections where representative works by the painters included in this book may be seen, will be found on page 69.

Lloyd O'Neil Pty Ltd
56 Claremont Street
South Yarra, Victoria, Australia

First published 1976
Second edition published 1980
Reprinted 1983
This edition published 1986
© Lloyd O'Neil Pty Ltd

This book was designed and set in Australia
and printed in Hong Kong through Bookbuilders Ltd

ISBN 0 85550 454 4

Page 2:
PLATE 2   Hans Heysen *A lord of the bush* (1908)

List of Plates

The Strangers in an Unfamiliar Land

The first European painters in Australia were never quite at home in the strange new land. They wished to show this strangeness to those who would otherwise never see it, or they wished to show its similarities, which they found strange too.

The earliest artists, usually loosely classified under the heading 'Colonial', included surveyors and explorers (Cook himself was no mean picture-maker), convicts — especially those transported for forgery which is, of course, an artistic pursuit — and those settlers who came with backgrounds that inclined them to paint, either as amateurs or, more rarely, as professionals.

Many of the early paintings of Australia were the work of convicts — notably Joseph Lycett, John Eyre, Thomas Watling and Thomas Wainewright. One of Australia's first professional artists, however, was a free man, Conrad Martens. Martens, the son of a German merchant in London, had been a topographical artist on Charles Darwin's ship *Beagle*. By the time he arrived in 1835, at the age of thirty-four, he was an artist of considerable ability, and not long after he settled in Sydney he opened a studio.

Martens was heir to the English tradition of watercolour painting and he was at his best in that medium. Romanticism was at its height when Martens arrived in Australia and all his works could be said to belong to this category. However, two years working with Darwin aboard the *Beagle* had taught him to record with exactitude, and while his Australian scenes have romantic overtones, the elements are correctly drawn — though perhaps exaggerated in the interests of the picturesque and the market. So in *Elizabeth Bay* (PLATE 4) the tree on the left is fantastic in size, the light is directed as though by a spotlight and the colour adds drama to the view of a great country house on Sydney Harbour over a century ago.

The early artists were primarily concerned with the landscape, for the exciting thing about the new land was its difference from the homeland, and this could best be conveyed graphically. Portraits were few, being outside the scope of surveyors, and still-lifes of this period are rare. One practitioner in both these forms, however, was Tasmania's first resident artist William Gould, who arrived in Hobart Town in December 1827 to serve a seven-year sentence for having 'by force of arms stolen one coat'. Gould was said to have been a porcelain painter at the Spode Factory but on arrival he was put to work at a brick-field and his artistic background did not come to the notice of officialdom until he forged a bank-note.

An artist such as Gould with, as far as we know, no formal training as a painter but with a background in the Staffordshire potteries, would have had little difficulty in producing a work such as *Flowers and fruit* (PLATE 3) but as might be expected from his background, the artist has a primitive touch. This shows clearly in his portraits, some of which may be seen in Tasmanian galleries.

The first professional artist with an established European reputation to settle in Australia was a Leicestershire farmer's son, John Glover. Glover had exhibited at the Royal Academy and the British Institution and was a founder and president of the Old Water Colour Society. He was sixty-three, much travelled and a comparatively wealthy man when he decided to migrate to Australia. Perhaps a desire to return to the soil and a wish to help his three sons already in Hobart prompted him to take his family to Tasmania where, soon after his arrival in 1831, he acquired land on the banks of the River Nile at Ben Lomond. He called his property 'Patterdale' in memory of a favourite locality on Lake Ullswater, Cumberland.

In painting *Patterdale* (PLATE 6) Glover revealed his knowledge of the French painter Claude Lorraine as he framed the picture with great trees right and left, threw a shadow from one across the foreground, and flooded the landscape with the golden light of a late afternoon in summer.

In the decades which followed, other visiting artists were to further expose the infant colonies to European tradition. One of the most accomplished was the Swiss, Nicholas Chevalier. In London he had built up a modest reputation as a watercolourist and lithographer, and in 1852 two of his paintings had been exhibited at the Royal Academy. About this time he also designed a fountain for Queen Victoria's Osborne House and the setting for the Koh-i-noor diamond in the British Crown.

Two years after his arrival in Melbourne Chevalier painted his *Self portrait* (PLATE 5). He was then only twenty-nine but he reveals his abilities clearly: this is no untrained, inexperienced colonial work. The dramatically-lit face merges with the surrounding gloom in a thoroughly Baroque manner, immediately suggesting Rembrandt as a major influence.

The goldfields, which had for a time attracted the attention of Chevalier, were sketched by an Englishman, William Strutt. He arrived in Melbourne in 1850 and not long afterwards was one of the first to join the Ballarat gold rush. Although he made a number of drawings of the diggers and diggings he apparently had little success as a prospector and before long resumed his original profession of artist. Strutt spent twelve years in Australia and was one of the first painters to produce 'national subjects' on a large scale. He made portraits of well-known local identities including John Pascoe Fawkner, the co-founder of Melbourne, and produced several canvases depicting aspects of the Burke and Wills expedition. In *Gold Diggers receiving a letter from home* (PLATE 7) we see Australia through alien eyes. Strutt, an Englishman with extensive training in Paris, painted like any European brought up in the neo-classical tradition. As Roberts did fifty years later, he sought to record history, painting those events that were all around him.

When the population began to rise sharply with the discovery of gold and improvement in trade, an increasing number of young people devoted themselves to art and proposed to live on the proceeds. Art schools of various kinds appeared, teaching well-established methods and, naturally, unsympathetic to such innovation as was appearing abroad. At length, however, rumours of progress and change reached Australia through new arrivals and returning students. Young painters gathered around these informed artists and gradually a new sophistication came about.

The principal influence from overseas was Louis Buvelot, a Swiss who had come to Australia in 1864. He profoundly influenced those young Australians who were drawn towards painting, encouraging them to study their subjects through their own vision. The work of Buvelot as illustrated in *The survey paddock* (PLATE 8) and *The Yarra Valley* (PLATE 9) is seen by many critics as a major influence in the development of what has been called the 'Australian School' of painting. He has been variously described as the 'first important artist to come to Australia' and 'the grandfather of Australian landscape painting'. Buvelot brought with him to Australia thirty years' experience in painting, and this shows in his work. Moreover, his introduction of the *plein-air* techniques favoured by the Barbizon school in Europe (much of the preliminary work for his paintings was done outdoors) caused him to have a far-reaching influence on the leading students of his day — Roberts, Streeton, McCubbin — who were to become the leaders of a new movement in Australian painting.

The Plates in Colour

11   PLATE 3   William Gould *Flowers and fruit* (1849)

PLATE 4   Conrad Martens *Elizabeth Bay and Elizabeth Bay House* (1838)

PLATE 5   Nicholas Chevalier *Self portrait* (1857)

PLATE 6   John Glover *Patterdale Farm* (c. 1840s)

PLATE 7   William Strutt *Gold Diggers receiving a letter from home* (c. 1860)

PLATE 8   Louis Buvelot   *The survey paddock* (1871)

17   PLATE 9   Louis Buvelot *The Yarra Valley, Melbourne* (1866)

PLATE 10   Tom Roberts   *Bourke Street (Allegro con brio)* (1885—86)

PLATE 11   Tom Roberts *Coming South* (1886)

PLATE 12   David Davies *A hot day* (1888)

The 'Golden Age' of Impressionism

Two of Buvelot's admirers became important in transmitting new ideas and enlarging the horizons of local artists who had not travelled: Tom Roberts in Melbourne and Julian Ashton in Sydney. Ashton founded the Sydney Art School, an institution in which many influential artists have since been taught; Roberts became the leader and inspiration of a group which established a series of artists' camps around Melbourne where the members worked at weekends or full time. The camp at Heidelberg gave a name to a whole movement, now known as the Heidelberg School or Australian Impressionism.

Roberts was born in Dorchester, England in 1856 and came to Australia at thirteen. In 1870 he enrolled in the Collingwood School of Design whose teachers included Thomas Clark, who had studied at the Royal Academy, and Louis Buvelot. Here, in 1875, Roberts won the drawing prize and subsequently enrolled in evening classes at the National Gallery of Victoria where he was to make friends with Louis Abrahams and Frederick McCubbin.

Some of Roberts' work was shown at the International Exhibition in Melbourne in 1880 and received favourable mention from the *Argus* critic James Smith. Encouraged by Clark, Roberts decided to study abroad. He sailed for Europe in 1881, spent four years at Royal Academy schools and made a walking tour through France and Spain, absorbing many new ideas from his European contemporaries.

In *Bourke Street* (PLATE 10), painted the year he returned to Melbourne, Roberts came close to those street scenes that occupied Monet and Pisarro. It is Roberts' Impressionism at its best. *Coming South* (PLATE 11) was begun on the voyage back to Australia. It has all the stock-in-trade of the academic subject picture but there is also light. This is no worn depiction of a tired theme; the whole scene is illuminated by a consciousness of light streaming from above, soft outdoor light, the light that was to make a new landscape possible in Australian painting.

Shortly after his return Roberts, Louis Abrahams and Frederick McCubbin established an artists' camp at the rural settlement of Box Hill, nine miles from Melbourne. McCubbin, who had begun to study painting while still working at his family's bakery, had a special fondness for the bushland in this area and many of his best-known works including probably *The lost child* (PLATE 15), *Down on his luck* (PLATE 14) and *A bush burial* (PLATE 18) were painted in this part of Melbourne. More than any painter before him, McCubbin understood the Australian bush. The sober colours so foreign to the European eye; the ordered chaos of the undergrowth; the stillness suggestive of indifference or even of hostility to the newcomer — McCubbin expressed these in the technique of the Australian Impressionists. In the popular taste of his time he made each picture tell a story: frequently one of the hardships of pioneering life.

Other artists joined the Box Hill group, among them a seventeen-year-old apprentice lithographer, Arthur Streeton. Streeton had met McCubbin at the National Gallery School where they were both students; it was he who initiated the Box Hill group's move to 'Eaglemont', an old house near the Yarra River at Heidelberg which was to become the group's new headquarters and, for a time, the home of the 'Heidelberg School'. Perhaps more than any of his contemporaries, Streeton's works are full of the blues and golds which he considered to be the characteristic colours of the Australian landscape and which have since come to be so closely associated with the Heidelberg painters. *Near Heidelberg* (PLATE 17) was painted at 'Eaglemont' in 1890.

Among the other artists who painted for a time at 'Eaglemont' was David Davies (PLATE 24), whose brother had been instrumental in obtaining the use of the house, and Charles Conder (PLATE 16) who in 1888 shared a city studio with Roberts. Many of the works produced at 'Eaglemont' formed the basis for the famous '9 x 5' exhibition which the group held in Melbourne in 1889 and which took its name from the fact that all the works had been painted on small panels of wood nine inches by five inches which were normally used for the lids of cigar boxes.

At the end of the summer of 1890 the camp at 'Eaglemont' disbanded. Conder prepared to go to Europe and Streeton went to Sydney where he was joined a year later by Roberts. Here the two established another artists' camp — Curlew Camp — near Mosman on a branch of Sydney Harbour, and for a time shared a studio in Sydney. During the next few years both painters travelled extensively in the New South Wales inland. On a previous trip Roberts had visited Brocklesby station, near Corowa in the Riverina, where he began one of his most famous paintings *Shearing the rams* (PLATE 20). Now resident in Sydney he continued to be obsessed with the necessity to capture the spirit of the pioneers, though their day was nearly past, and in 1891 he painted *The breakaway* (PLATE 22). Here the heat and dust of the Australian Outback permeate the scene; the excitement of the incident is communicated. It is hard to credit that the picture was assembled from notes and sketches, and that the foreground horseman was posed in the studio astride a vaulting horse.

In Sydney, however, Roberts was perhaps better known as a portrait painter. His *Portrait of Florence* (PLATE 21) painted in 1898 was one of the many studies, especially those of women, which would prove him a painter of the first rank if all his other work had been destroyed. During the last years of the century he spent a good deal of his time on portrait work, his subjects including such notables as Sir Henry Parkes, Viscount Hampden and Earl Beauchamp.

Streeton, meanwhile, had exhibited a number of the paintings he made at Curlew Camp, but without success, and he too travelled in the hinterland. 'I intend to go straight inland,' he wrote to Roberts '. . . and stay there two or three years and create something entirely new and try and translate some of the great hidden poetry that I know is here but have not seen or felt. . .' One of his favourite regions was the Blue Mountains, west of Sydney, and it was on one of his trips here that he painted *'Fire's on'* (PLATE 23) depicting the body of a workman caught by a blast, being carried out of the tunnel's mouth. Five years later, after several trips back to Melbourne, he visited the upper reaches of the Hawkesbury River to paint *'The purple noon's transparent might'* (PLATE 13), which was sold to the National Gallery of Victoria at his first one-man exhibition in Melbourne late in 1896.

Both Streeton and Roberts were later to travel to Europe, and before long the excitement of Australian Impressionism waned. It was hardly Impressionism as invented in France, though several innovations were common to each. (One was the rapid sketch-like character of the works; another was the emphasis placed on capturing the first impression of the subject — it was generally painted 'on the spot' so there could be no working-over or underpainting in the studio.) But the features which lifted the Heidelberg School above mere painting were not technical. A conviction that a new art was emerging raised the participants to great heights of emotional excitement. Their landscapes glow with the vision of a wonderful world exalted beyond any plebeian account of the ground and growth that lay before them.

PLATE 13   Arthur Streeton *'The purple noon's transparent might'* (1896)

PLATE 14   Frederick McCubbin *Down on his luck* (1889)

PLATE 15   Frederick McCubbin *Lost (1886)*

PLATE 16   Charles Conder *Springtime* (1888)

PLATE 17   Arthur Streeton *Near Heidelberg* (1890)

PLATE 18   Frederick McCubbin *A bush burial* (1890)

PLATE 19   Julian Ashton *The prospector* (1889)

PLATE 20   Tom Roberts *Shearing the rams* (1890)

PLATE 21   Tom Roberts *Portrait of Florence* (1898)

PLATE 22   Tom Roberts *The breakaway* (1891)

PLATE 23   Arthur Streeton *'Fire's on', Lapstone Tunnel* (1891)

34 PLATE 24 David Davies *A Summer evening* (c. 1896)

The French Influence on Young Painters

Although the Impressionism of the Heidelberg School attracted much attention, few of its proponents were able to make a living from their art; one by one they left Australia, some to study and seek an audience abroad, some never to return. They were followed to Europe by the new generation of Australian painters, many of whom were to be strongly influenced by their French contemporaries.

Emmanuel Phillips Fox was born in Melbourne in 1865 and began his studies at the Melbourne gallery school. In 1887 he went to Paris where one of his teachers was Gerome, whose dictum '. . . in painting the first thing to look for is the general impression of colour' had appeared on the catalogue of the Melbourne '9 x 5' exhibition. On his return to Australia he joined with Tudor St George Tucker to establish the Melbourne Art School where the Impressionist ideals and *plein-air* approach were taught. The two also conducted a summer school for painters at 'Charterisville', an old mansion not far from the original Heidelberg group's headquarters, which was to become the centre of an artists' colony for five generations of Australian painters. (One of the first to live there was Walter Withers.) *The art students* (PLATE 25) was first exhibited at the Victorian Art Society in 1895 but Phillips Fox could find no buyer and the painting was still unsold at his death twenty-five years later.

The work of Phillips Fox reveals, to a much greater degree than that of his contemporaries, the influence of French Impressionism. It was an influence shown not only in his manner of painting but in his choice of subjects, for while Phillips Fox painted the Australian landscape his paintings are more truly characterised by their preoccupation with sunlight and water, beautiful women, flowers and food.

In 1902 he returned to Europe and eventually settled in Paris where, in 1908, he was elected an associate of the New Salon. *The arbour* (PLATE 26), painted during his second sojourn in France, is a picture that illustrates his debt to the French Impressionists, and especially to Renoir. He displays the same love of dappled sunlight and the glow of light reflected from surrounding objects, and the subject matter could have been assembled from the works of Renoir himself. Like all the Impressionists he draws on a leisured life in which it is always a summer afternoon, gently happy. There is nothing exotic about his work, nor is there anything particularly Australian about it. *The lesson* (PLATE 27) was executed three years before the artist's death in 1915. A child reads from a book and her mother sits beside her, while the sunny light from the garden filters through voile curtains from the windows behind. The colours are pastel; rosy light and grey-green shade; the technique approaches pointilism. There is a charm about every aspect of this painting: the subject, the setting (note the peacock-eyed cover on the couch and the oval-framed portrait on the wall which date the decor); the colour — even the weather.

The same year that Phillips Fox made his second trip to Europe, Hugh Ramsay, who was twelve years his junior, painted *Jeanne* (PLATE 29). Ramsay came to Australia in 1878, when he was a year old. He, too, studied at the Melbourne gallery school and in 1900 travelled to Paris with his fellow student, George Lambert. Ramsay was greatly influenced by Velasquez and in company with Lambert frequently copied the Spanish master's works in the Louvre. His own talent, however, was indisputable; in the 1902 exhibition at the New Salon four of the five works he submitted were accepted —

a rare accolade for a young unknown artist. In *Jeanne* the tonal method of Velasquez is predominant, though the arrangement of the model owes something to Whistler. The mood is quiet, the pose is expressive of patient watchfulness. This is helped by the arrangement, strictly frontal in a very shallow space, though slightly asymmetrical, with the minimum of accessories: floor, curtain and chair. But few observers will look at the surroundings. What grips the imagination is the character revealed in the face. It is extraordinary that this young man of twenty-five should be able to paint the woman-to-come in the face of the child.

In *The sisters* (PLATE 28), unlike *Jeanne*, the bravura we associate with Sargent is evident — it would even be dominant were it not for the heads. In spite of the great areas of white and near-white that by themselves could almost form an abstract painting, we find our attention held by the two Edwardian ladies. The great personal achievement of Ramsay is again demonstrated. He could look into his sitters and find a personality which he made clear by means far more subtle than superficial resemblance. When Ramsay died in Melbourne from tuberculosis at the age of twenty-nine Australia lost one of her most brilliant and promising painters.

The most fashionable portrait painter of Ramsay's time, however, was John Longstaff, yet another graduate of the Melbourne gallery school. In 1887 he won the gallery's first travelling scholarship and the following year went to Europe where he spent the next six years. He returned to Australia in 1894 with an established reputation as a portrait painter and before long obtained commissions to paint a number of leading figures, including the writer and poet Henry Lawson (PLATE 32). Longstaff by that time (1900) could produce a likeness with great facility. His portrait of Lawson, then aged thirty-three, shows a conventionally-posed young man, attractive in appearance, with the eyes of a poet and fine creative hands. Unlike most portraits of the time this carries the subject's name and the date in large Art Nouveau letters.

Early in the twentieth century the theories of painting which had so strongly influenced the Melbourne school received a strong challenge. Max Meldrum, a former student of Frederick McCubbin, caused a sensation by preaching a gospel of strict tonal painting. His theories — later promoted through his own art school, founded in 1913 — were in strong conflict with those of the Heidelberg School and between them these two outlooks provided much of the basis of Australian art before post-Impressionism arrived in the thirties. Meldrum's *Portrait of the artist's mother* (PLATE 31) illustrates at one and the same time his theories concerning painting and his ability to transcend them. His belief was that painting consisted of copying the tonal values of the subject, area by area, on to a canvas: when the painted area matched the equivalent area of the subject the picture was finished. A camera could do no less. Yet it was Meldrum's departures from this simple formula that lifted him above his scores of imitators. *Portrait of the artist's mother* is a presentation of those items that matter, with a complete suppression of irrelevant detail. The hair and dress are completely lost in the background: all that remains are the face and a faint suggestion of collar and blouse. Colour is reduced to a beautifully-modulated flesh-tint. It is the sympathetic treatment of the beloved features that lifts this painting above the run of Meldrum's work.

At least one of Meldrum's contemporaries, however, remained unaffected by debates on the theories of painting. Hans Heysen was a remarkable example of single-minded devotion to one ideal. While most artists of his period vacillated between Australia and Europe, and between landscapes and subject pictures, Heysen settled in the village of Hahndorf in the Adelaide hills and spent the rest of his long life painting the surrounding landscape. Indisputably the best-known and most admired painter of the Australian eucalypts, Heysen was the first Australian artist to capture the beauty and majesty of these native trees. Unfortunately his imitators have built his methods into a formula and it is not always easy to see his work through unprejudiced eyes. *A lord of the bush* (PLATE 2) is a portrait of a tree obviously painted by one who loved it. It is one of his earlier works and his draughtsmanship was superb.

PLATE 25   E. Phillips Fox *The art students* (1895)

PLATE 26   E. Phillips Fox *The arbour* (c. 1911)

PLATE 27   E. Phillips Fox *The lesson* (c. 1912)

PLATE 28   Hugh Ramsay *The sisters* (1904)

PLATE 29   Hugh Ramsay *Jeanne* (1902)

PLATE 30   Elioth Gruner *Spring frost: Emu Plains* (1919)

PLATE 31   Max Meldrum *Portrait of the artist's mother* (c. 1912)

Australian Painting after Heidelberg

In the first decades of the twentieth century widely different influences could be seen in Australian painting. On the one hand, Arthur Streeton and Tom Roberts were still painting the Australian landscape (though it is generally conceded that their later work lacked the freshness of approach and inspiration that marked the high point of the Heidelberg school); at the same time, European post-Impressionism began to strongly influence the works of some younger artists.

But among the significant painters of the period there were also those who developed highly individual styles that owed little to prevailing trends of the time.

Jesse Jewhurst Hilder began studying painting at night at Julian Ashton's. In 1909, when he was twenty-eight, he contracted tuberculosis, which led him to give up his job in a bank and spend the rest of his relatively short life painting full-time. He was a prolific worker but the relatively low prices he received for this work forced him to live in near poverty.

Hilder's proficient watercolour *The crossroads* (PLATE 35) is remarkable in view of his isolation from other painters in the medium. While many young ladies were producing genteel watercolour pictures of picturesque subjects in the early years of this century, very few artists in Australia made serious contributions to the art, since watercolour was generally considered a poor relation to oil paint. Nevertheless it had been a significant part of the Romantic movement of the nineteenth century, and Hilder's work must be seen as one of the last manifestations of Romanticism. His pleasant landscapes just avoid being merely pretty: they always verge on the sentimental, the colour is appealing, the subjects nostalgic. Yet mere prettiness is avoided by a fine sense of colour; the apparent subject is not the real point of the picture, which is an arrangement of forms in space, despite the atmospheric effects of light. And those qualities peculiar to watercolour are wonderfully exploited.

A vastly different worker in watercolour was Norman Lindsay, who became one of the best-known of all Australian artists though there is little in his work which is distinctively Australian in character. He was born in 1879 at Creswick, Victoria, into a family which was to be almost wholly preoccupied with the arts: his brothers Lionel, Percy and Daryl all became well-known as painters and illustrators, and his sister Ruby worked in black and white.

Lindsay had received some lessons in painting from Walter Withers when the artist visited Creswick, but he had had no real formal training when he went to Melbourne at the age of sixteen to join his elder brother Lionel. Nevertheless, he made a living, and in 1901 got a job as an artist on the *Bulletin* in Sydney.

During the next years Lindsay spent much of his time writing: his most famous children's book, *The Magic Pudding*, appeared in 1918 with illustrations by the author, and he completed the novels *Redheap* and *Saturdee*.

Throughout the 1920s he occupied himself with painting and sculpture. Several of his paintings were included in the 1923 exhibition of Australian art held at Burlington House in London, and in 1930 a special edition of the magazine *Art in Australia* was devoted to his work. Lindsay's themes, however, so offended the morals of the time that the magazine was prosecuted for obscenity; the case was dismissed but Lindsay was so disgusted at the commotion that he went to America.

45

PLATE 32   John Longstaff *Henry Lawson* (1900)

On his return he settled at the house at Springwood in the Blue Mountains, west of Sydney, which was to be his home and studio for the rest of his life. He remained a controversial figure almost until his death in 1969 at the age of ninety.

Norman Lindsay's world is very much a dream-world, both exotic and erotic. He has a great deal in common with Watteau. The same misty gardens furnished with the same classical ornaments — urns and balustrades, fountains and the occasional column — are peopled by voluptuous women and leering men, all with maniacal eyes. The compositions are splendidly executed, usually as etchings or water-colours. *The merchant of robes* (PLATE 33) might be from the Arabian Nights. It has little to do with the Australian scene or with the life of the intellect, but it provides an excellent excuse for a demonstration of the artist's highly skilled handling of watercolour.

Only three years before Lindsay painted *The merchant of robes* Penleigh Boyd had painted *Breath of Spring* (PLATE 34), a work in complete contrast. Boyd was born in England, the son of two well-known artists and a member of one of Australia's most famous artistic families. His brief career was devoted to landscape painting, and he had the reputation of being 'the only artist who could paint wattle'. *Breath of Spring* could have been by Whistler, perhaps as a 'Symphony in green and gold', for Penleigh Boyd had the rare ability to make unlikely colours sing, and his sensitivity helped him to escape the banal. He seems to have by-passed the Heidelberg School yet his freshness and the sense of weather and light that permeates his work link him to the spirit of the nineties.

For a time, during the twenties, the techniques of Impressionism enjoyed a return to fashion. One of its leading proponents was New Zealand-born Elioth Gruner, a student of Julian Ashton's. *Spring Frost* (PLATE 30) earned Gruner the Wynne Prize in 1919 and is typical of his early work. Light was Gruner's first preoccupation: especially morning light, and especially subjects seen against the light. His tonal training contributed to the success of these paintings and so did his technique, which was to cover the canvas evenly with small brush strokes in the manner of Davies.

Later, Gruner was to modify his approach to place more importance on form than on the effects of atmosphere which had earlier attracted him. In *Bellingen pastoral* (PLATE 38) painted in 1937, we see Gruner at his best. The lessons of the past are learned and the temptations of the twenties put aside. The countryside is still a little too tidy, the rules have been followed so carefully that they show, but there is a lyricism and a delight in the subject that appeals. We share the peaceful afternoon and the calm routine of pastoral life. It would never do to paint the Australian desert thus, but it suits those parts of the country which, like the English landscape, have been 'patted into shape'. The magic of the Heidelberg painters has gone, but there remains a hint of their dream of 'golden days' which Gruner was just too late to share.

Perhaps the best-known painter to emerge during the thirties was William Dobell. Dobell was born in Newcastle in 1899 and after studies in drawing became articled to a local architect. At the end of his apprenticeship in 1929 he went to Sydney, worked as an architectural designer, and attended evening classes at Julian Ashton's. In the same year, after winning the Society of Artists' Travelling Scholarship and several other prizes, he went to London and enrolled at the Slade School of Art to study drawing. Here, in 1930, he won first prize for life painting and subsequently went to Holland where he spent three months studying the old masters, particularly Rembrandt, Goya and Daumier.

The boy at the basin (PLATE 37) is a small picture, painted in London just before Dobell's individuality began to emerge. It is quiet and retiring: nothing is done for effect. Dobell had already begun a study of Rembrandt's works but here we are reminded of other Dutch masters — especially Vermeer with his serene, impersonal vision and his room so beautifully bathed in cool revealing light. Dobell's colours are subdued and delightful, but above all it is his remarkable ability to use paint that makes this work a taste of things to come. Here the texture makes towelling, there it is enamel, now metal, and now flesh, yet it is always paint. The whole is a piece of student work, carefully feeling its way among the possibilities, but what a student!

PLATE 33   Norman Lindsay *The merchant of robes* (1922)

PLATE 34   Penleigh Boyd *Breath of Spring* (1919)

48   PLATE 35   J. J. Hilder *The crossroads* (1910)

J.J. HILDER
1910

PLATE 36   Sali Herman *The Law Court* (c. 1946)

PLATE 37   William Dobell *The boy at the basin* (1932)

PLATE 38   Elioth Gruner *Bellingen pastoral* (1937)

PLATE 39   William Dobell *The sleeping Greek* (1936)

PLATE 40   Arthur Boyd *Irrigation lake, Wimmera* (c. 1948)

New Visions in an Ancient Land

In 1936, four years after *The boy at the basin* and while he was still in London, Dobell painted *The sleeping Greek* (PLATE 39). Now the texture and the drawing are both freer, the colour less dependent on reality and more evocative. Dobell now reveals an interest in the people he paints: there is little in *The boy at the basin* to concern us about the model himself, but this 'sleeping Greek' is a particular Greek, a waiter with whom Dobell became acquainted, and who posed for several other pictures.

Though Dobell had entered the Archibald Prize since 1940, he was not successful in the competition until 1943 when he entered *Brian Penton, The billy boy* and *Joshua Smith* — any one of which, it has been said, could have won the award. However, when the prize was ultimately awarded to the portrait of Dobell's friend and fellow-painter Joshua Smith, the decision provoked a storm of controversy. This culminated in a court action brought by two of the unsuccessful entrants who claimed that the Art Gallery of New South Wales had breached the terms of the prize by awarding it for a work which, it was argued, was a caricature.

Although the action was lost, Dobell was greatly upset by the ensuing publicity; he suffered a nervous breakdown which caused his left leg to be paralysed for a time and for twelve months he stopped painting. *Helena Rubinstein* (PLATE 41), a later work completed about 1957, shows the sitter as the strong decisive creator of a huge industrial empire. Alert intelligence dominates and the technique matches: swift, bold brushwork states exactly what has to be said.

While Dobell was attracting public interest with his portraits, his contemporary Russell Drysdale was introducing Australians to a new vision of the outback. He was one of the first to adopt the outback as a subject and indeed it has been said that his paintings of the desolate fringe of the interior are better known to most Australians than the outback itself.

After his schooling Drysdale became an overseer on his father's property and it was only by chance that he came to make painting a career. In 1932 he developed a defect in his left eye and was forced to go to Melbourne for treatment. Here he took to sketching to fill in time, and after his work had been shown to Daryl Lindsay and the teacher George Bell their encouragement led him to make a trip to Europe where he subsequently studied both the old masters and the post-Impressionists. *Two children* (PLATE 43) is rare among Drysdale's paintings in that it gives no hint of place. It is obviously set in the outback, but no distant houses, no unpaved street, no stone mountain or waterhole hint at a setting. There is only yellow sand under a dusty sky: the colour suggests aridity but even the light is soft. The children are monumental, no less figures in a landscape than are works by Henry Moore, and they share his simplicity of form, together with that of Modigliani. This form is suggested by conventional techniques: the teaching of George Bell is still evident.

Sofala (PLATE 42) shows the small mining town in New South Wales. Once crowded with life, it died, like so many Australian towns, when the gold ran out, leaving behind monuments to reasonable aspiration. Drysdale is on the whole an accurate reporter of the world he watches but there is tension in his burning colour and in his elongated poles and pillars, and the empty windows waiting for someone long dead. No living thing is to be seen, human or animal, not even vegetation. As in so much recent painting Mannerism is come again, and Drysdale has profited from those forms of Surrealism current in the thirties.

In the fifties Drysdale's interest turned more and more to the Australian aborigines. At first the familiar landscapes were peopled by appropriately clad or unclad figures, perhaps more realistically painted than the setting behind them. Latterly these figures have often been set into a background which no longer appears as a landscape, but as rocks or, as in *Mangula* (PLATE 45), the grave posts of Melville Island. The colours are still reds, browns and yellows, but less is made of their relationship with reality. The canvas has become a pattern of angular and rounded forms: it is almost a step towards abstraction.

Reports of European post-Impressionism began to permeate art schools in the thirties. By then a few artists had already made tentative experiments in this manner, mostly based on reproductions and books from abroad. In Melbourne a school was founded by George Bell and Arnold Shore to teach the post-Impressionist philosophy and methods; Bell's students, at one time or another, included Drysdale, Sali Herman (PLATE 36) and many other well-known artists. The post-Impressionist movement gave birth to a group which eventually became the Contemporary Art Society, while in Sydney similar developments were associated with Julian Ashton's school and encouraged by such older artists as Roy de Maistre and Roland Wakelin.

At first there was great opposition to these revolutionary methods, seen as a threat by those adherents of older traditions. But the social disruptions caused by World War Two helped develop a greater tolerance and from 1945 onwards a new generation began to advance very different ideas of art, the more readily acceptable since the whole social structure of Australia was changing also. Sidney Nolan, Arthur Boyd, Leonard French and many others began their careers at this time. Exposed to a flood of prints from overseas, to loan exhibitions freely circulating between the world's principal galleries, and with foreign travel more readily available, the provincial attitude which had acted as a spur to some and a brake to many earlier painters was no longer tenable.

Nolan and Boyd, in particular, have been responsible for an unprecedented overseas interest in Australian painting. Both were influenced by their contact with the Contemporary Art Society, the group of young radical painters and writers whose members also included Albert Tucker, John Percival, John Reed, Max Harris and Geoffrey Dutton. Both brought a completely new vision to the Australian landscape. Boyd's *Irrigation lake, Wimmera* (PLATE 40), painted about 1948, makes obvious the Impressionists' discovery that Australia is gold and blue. Nolan's *Pretty Polly Mine* (PLATE 44), painted at about the same time, is one of a series of landscapes in which Nolan's surrealism plays a part: clear and unclear areas are inexplicable save that they strengthen awareness, and some monstrous image floats above — a bird, a photograph, a machine. Here it is Polly herself, flying huge over the strange mine machinery which looks rather like a river steam boat stranded in the desert.

Like Nolan, Leonard French and Robert Dickerson had no substantial formal training in painting. French spent five years as a signwriter: in his paintings, such as *Death and Transfiguration* (PLATE 48), the most obvious and appealing quality is decoration. Great glowing forms shine brightly from rich dark grounds, or glow dimly through layer upon layer of glaze. They abound with symbols, some personal, some universal, and are far from being the purely decorative arrangements they first appear. Dickerson's theme in *Tired Man* (PLATE 46) is the lonely individual. No more background is provided than is absolutely necessary: in this case a bench and green mound. Dickerson makes a solid symbol dispassionately. There is no involvement, no compassion, no anger. Here is a tired man. He is lonely.

Loneliness, of a different nature, is suggested also in Lawrence Daws' *Sungazer III* (PLATE 47). On a first casual inspection this large and decorative canvas appears to be an abstraction. Then the sungazer resolves himself, standing on the right, ill-defined as though he stood for all men or any man. The painting makes a fundamental statement about the Australian outback where only the sun lives in its own right and all other life is there on sufferance.

The often hostile, often intimidatory character of the Australian landscape emerges as a persistent theme in Australian painting, linking painters of such different periods and styles as Drysdale and McCubbin and indeed stretching back to the earliest colonial painters who first looked with wonderment and sometimes apprehension at a vast and empty continent.

PLATE 41   William Dobell *Helena Rubinstein* (c. 1957)

PLATE 42   Russell Drysdale *Sofala* (1947)

58   PLATE 43   Russell Drysdale *Two children* (c. 1946)

PLATE 44   Sidney Nolan *Pretty Polly Mine* (1948)

60

PLATE 45   Russell Drysdale *Mangula* (1961)

PLATE 46   Robert Dickerson *Tired man* (c. 1957)

63   PLATE 47   Lawrence Daws *Sungazer III* (1961)

64   PLATE 48   Leonard French *Death and transfiguration* 1961

Details of the Paintings

1 WALTER WITHERS (1857—1914)
Tranquil Winter 1895
Oil on canvas 75.5 x 122.5
National Gallery of Victoria
Purchased 1895

2 HANS HEYSEN (1877—1968)
A lord of the bush 1908
Oil on canvas 134.5 x 104
National Gallery of Victoria
Felton Bequest 1908
Reproduced by courtesy of David Heysen

3 WILLIAM GOULD (1801—1853)
Flowers and fruit 1849
Oil on canvas 66 x 77
Art Gallery of New South Wales
Purchased 1956

4 CONRAD MARTENS (1801—1878)
Elizabeth Bay and Elizabeth Bay House 1838
Watercolour 44 x 63
National Gallery of Victoria

5 NICHOLAS CHEVALIER (1828—1902)
Self portrait 1857
Oil on board 35 x 25.5
Art Gallery of New South Wales
Bequest of Mrs Nicholas Chevalier 1919

6 JOHN GLOVER (1767—1849)
Patterdale Farm c. 1840s
Oil on canvas 77 x 114.5
Reproduced by courtesy of the owners,
Mesdames J. W. Butler and L. Nye

7 WILLIAM STRUTT (1825—1915)
Gold Diggers receiving a letter from home
c. 1860
Oil on canvas 91.5 x 72.5
Art Gallery of New South Wales

8 LOUIS BUVELOT (1814—1888)
The survey paddock 1871
Oil on canvas 25.5 x 35.5
National Gallery of Victoria
Presented by John H. Connell 1914

9 LOUIS BUVELOT (1814—1888)
The Yarra Valley, Melbourne 1866
Oil on canvas 57 x 71
National Gallery of Victoria
Felton Bequest 1934

10 TOM ROBERTS (1856—1931)
Bourke Street (Allegro con brio) 1885—86
Oil on canvas 51 x 76.5
National Library of Australia

11 TOM ROBERTS (1856—1931)
Coming South 1886
Oil on canvas 64 x 50.5
National Gallery of Victoria
Gift of Colonel Aubrey H. L. Gibson, 1967,
in memory of John and Anne Gibson,
settlers, 1887

12 DAVID DAVIES (1862—1939)
A hot day 1888
Oil on canvas 60.5 x 91.5
National Gallery of Victoria
Felton Bequest 1937

13 ARTHUR STREETON (1867—1943)
'The purple noon's transparent might' 1896
Oil on canvas 122 x 122
National Gallery of Victoria
Reproduced by courtesy of Oliver Streeton

14 FREDERICK McCUBBIN (1855—1917)
Down on his luck 1889
Oil on canvas 114.5 x 152.5
Western Australian Art Gallery
Purchased 1896

15 FREDERICK McCUBBIN (1855—1917)
Lost 1886
Oil on canvas 114.5 x 72.5
National Gallery of Victoria
Felton Bequest 1940

16 CHARLES CONDER (1868—1909)
Springtime 1888
Oil on canvas 44.1 x 59
National Gallery of Victoria
Felton Bequest 1914

17 ARTHUR STREETON (1867—1943)
Near Heidelberg 1890
Oil on canvas 52 x 39
National Gallery of Victoria
Felton Bequest 1943
Reproduced by courtesy of Oliver Streeton

18 FREDERICK McCUBBIN (1855—1917)
A bush burial 1890
Oil on canvas 122.5 x 224.5
Geelong Art Gallery

19 JULIAN ASHTON (1851—1942)
The prospector 1889
Oil on canvas 213 x 117
Art Gallery of New South Wales
Purchased 1889

20 TOM ROBERTS (1856—1931)
Shearing the rams 1890
Oil on canvas 119 x 180
National Gallery of Victoria
Felton Bequest 1932

21 TOM ROBERTS (1856—1931)
Portrait of Florence 1898
Oil on canvas 66 x 38
Art Gallery of New South Wales
Florence Turner Blake Bequest Fund

22 TOM ROBERTS (1856—1931)
The breakaway 1891
Oil on canvas 137.5 x 168
The Art Gallery of South Australia

23 ARTHUR STREETON (1867—1943)
'Fire's on', Lapstone Tunnel 1891

Oil on canvas 184 x 122.5
Art Gallery of New South Wales
Reproduced by courtesy of Oliver Streeton

24 DAVID DAVIES (1862—1939)
A Summer evening c. 1896
Oil on canvas mounted on hardboard
71 x 91
Art Gallery of New South Wales

25 E. PHILLIPS FOX (1865—1915)
The art students 1895
Oil on canvas 183 x 114.5
Art Gallery of New South Wales

26 E. PHILLIPS FOX (1865—1915)
The arbour c. 1911
Oil on canvas 190 x 230.5
National Gallery of Victoria
Felton Bequest 1916

27 E. PHILLIPS FOX (1865—1915)
The lesson c. 1912
Oil on canvas 182 x 112
National Gallery of Victoria
Felton Bequest 1925

28 HUGH RAMSAY (1877—1906)
The sisters 1904
Oil on canvas 125 x 145
Art Gallery of New South Wales

29 HUGH RAMSAY (1877—1906)
Jeanne 1902
Oil on canvas 129.5 x 89
National Gallery of Victoria
Lent by Mrs J. Wicking

30 ELIOTH GRUNER (1882—1939)
Spring frost: Emu Plains 1919
Oil on canvas 131 x 178.5
Art Gallery of New South Wales
Gift of F. G. White 1939
Reproduced by courtesy of
Perpetual Trustee Co. Ltd

31 MAX MELDRUM (1875—1955)
Portrait of the artist's mother c. 1912
Oil on canvas 61 x 49.5
National Gallery of Victoria
Felton Bequest 1913

32 JOHN LONGSTAFF (1862—1941)
Henry Lawson 1900
Oil on canvas 91.5 x 78.5
Art Gallery of New South Wales

33 NORMAN LINDSAY (1879–1969)
The merchant of robes 1922
Watercolour 45 x 44
Art Gallery of New South Wales

34 PENLEIGH BOYD (1890–1923)
Breath of Spring 1919
Oil on canvas 122 x 153.5
National Gallery of Victoria
Felton Bequest 1919

35 J. J. HILDER (1881–1916)
The crossroads 1910
Watercolour 70 x 49.5
Art Gallery of New South Wales
Dr George A. Brookes Bequest

36 SALI HERMAN (b. 1898)
The Law Court c. 1946
Oil on canvas 61 x 81.5
National Gallery of Victoria
Felton Bequest 1946

37 WILLIAM DOBELL (1899–1970)
The boy at the basin 1932
Oil on wood panel 40.5 x 33
Art Gallery of New South Wales

38 ELIOTH GRUNER (1882–1939)
Bellingen pastoral 1937
Oil on canvas 62.5 x 75
National Gallery of Victoria
Felton Bequest 1940
Reproduced by courtesy of Perpetual
Trustee Co. Ltd

39 WILLIAM DOBELL (1899–1970)
The sleeping Greek 1936
Oil on canvas, on masonite 38 x 33
Art Gallery of New South Wales
Gift of the Society of Artists in memory of
Sydney Ure Smith 1950

40 ARTHUR BOYD (b. 1920)
Irrigation lake, Wimmera c. 1948
Resin and tempera on hardboard 81 x 122
National Gallery of Victoria
Purchased 1950

41 WILLIAM DOBELL (1899–1970)
Helena Rubinstein c. 1957
Oil on hardboard 98 x 99
National Gallery of Victoria
Felton Bequest 1964

42 RUSSELL DRYSDALE (b. 1912)
Sofala 1947
Oil on canvas 72 x 93
Art Gallery of New South Wales

43 RUSSELL DRYSDALE (b. 1912)
Two children c. 1946
Oil on canvas on composition board 61 x 51
National Gallery of Victoria
Purchased 1946

44 SIDNEY NOLAN (b. 1917)
Pretty Polly Mine 1948
Synthetic enamel on hardboard 91 x 122
Art Gallery of New South Wales

45 RUSSELL DRYSDALE (b. 1912)
Mangula 1961
Oil on canvas 183 x 122
Art Gallery of New South Wales
Florence Turner Blake Bequest Fund

46 ROBERT DICKERSON (b. 1924)
Tired man c. 1957
Synthetic enamel on hardboard 137 x 152.5
National Gallery of Victoria
Purchased 1957

47 LAWRENCE DAWS (b. 1927)
Sungazer III 1961
Oil on canvas 173 x 167
National Gallery of Victoria
A. R. Henderson Bequest 1963

48 LEONARD FRENCH (b. 1928)
Death and transfiguration 1961
Enamel, collage and gold leaf on hessian
on hardboard 122 x 138
Art Gallery of New South Wales
Sir Charles Lloyd Jones Bequest Fund 1962

Artists in Public Collections

JULIAN ASHTON
New South Wales, Victorian, South Australian, Queensland and Western Australian State galleries; Geelong and Newcastle galleries.

ARTHUR BOYD
New South Wales, South Australian, Queensland, Western Australian and (especially) Victorian State galleries; Bendigo gallery; University of Western Australia.

PENLEIGH BOYD
New South Wales, Victorian, South Australian and Queensland State galleries; Bendigo, Mildura and Castlemaine galleries; National Collection, Canberra.

LOUIS BUVELOT
New South Wales, Victorian, South Australian, Queensland and Western Australian State galleries; Bendigo, Geelong and Newcastle galleries.

NICHOLAS CHEVALIER
New South Wales, Victorian, South Australian and Queensland State galleries; Ballarat gallery.

CHARLES CONDER
New South Wales, Victorian, South Australian, Queensland and Western Australian State galleries; Bendigo, Newcastle, Ballarat and Geelong galleries.

DAVID DAVIES
New South Wales, Victorian and South Australian State galleries; Ballarat gallery.

LAWRENCE DAWS
New South Wales, Victorian, Queensland, Western Australian, Tasmanian and (especially) South Australian State galleries; Ballarat and Mildura galleries; University of Western Australia.

ROBERT DICKERSON
New South Wales, Victorian, South Australian, Queensland, Western Australian and Tasmanian State galleries; Ballarat gallery; Australian National University, Canberra.

WILLIAM DOBELL
Victorian, South Australian, Queensland, Tasmanian and (especially) New South Wales and Western Australian State galleries; Bendigo and Ballarat galleries; Australian National War Memorial, Canberra.

RUSSELL DRYSDALE
Victorian, South Australian, Queensland, Western Australian, Tasmanian and (especially) New South Wales State galleries; Geelong, Newcastle and Ballarat galleries.

LEONARD FRENCH
New South Wales, Victorian, Queensland, Western Australian and Tasmanian State galleries; Ballarat gallery; University of Western Australia.

E. PHILLIPS FOX
New South Wales, Victorian, South Australian, Queensland, Western Australian and Tasmanian State galleries; Geelong and Ballarat galleries; National Collection, Canberra.

JOHN GLOVER
Victorian, Tasmanian and South Australian State galleries; Launceston and Ballarat galleries.

WILLIAM GOULD
New South Wales, Victorian and Tasmanian State galleries; Queen Victoria Museum, Hobart; Launceston gallery; Entally National House, Tasmania.

ELIOTH GRUNER
Victorian, South Australian, Queensland, Western Australian and (especially) New South Wales State galleries; Newcastle, Castlemaine and Geelong galleries; Mitchell Library, Sydney.

SALI HERMAN
New South Wales, Victorian, Queensland, Western Australian and Tasmanian State galleries; Bendigo, Geelong, Newcastle and Ballarat galleries; Australian National War Memorial, Canberra.

HANS HEYSEN
New South Wales, Victorian, Queensland, Western Australian, Tasmanian and (especially) South Australian State galleries; Bendigo, Geelong, Newcastle, Ballarat, Mildura and Castlemaine galleries; University of Western Australia.

J. J. HILDER
New South Wales, Victorian, South Australian, Queensland, Western Australian and Tasmanian State galleries; Bendigo, Geelong, Newcastle, Ballarat and Castlemaine galleries.

NORMAN LINDSAY
New South Wales, Victorian, South Australian, Queensland, Western Australian and Tasmanian State galleries; Bendigo, Castlemaine and (especially) Ballarat galleries.

JOHN LONGSTAFF
New South Wales (22 works), Victorian, South Australian, Queensland, Western Australian and Tasmanian State galleries; Bendigo, Geelong, Ballarat and Castlemaine galleries; universities of Melbourne and Sydney; Australian National War Memorial, Canberra; National Collection, Canberra.

CONRAD MARTENS
New South Wales, Victorian, South Australian and Queensland State galleries; Bendigo, Newcastle and Launceston galleries; Dixson gallery and Mitchell Library, Sydney; National Library, Canberra.

FREDERICK McCUBBIN
New South Wales, Victorian, South Australian, Queensland and Western Australian State galleries; Bendigo, Geelong, Ballarat and Castlemaine galleries.

MAX MELDRUM
New South Wales, Victorian, South Australian, Queensland, Western Australian and Tasmanian State galleries; Newcastle, Ballarat, Castlemaine and Shepparton galleries; National Collection, Canberra.

SIDNEY NOLAN
Victorian, South Australian, Queensland, Western Australian, Tasmanian and (especially) New South Wales State galleries; Ballarat gallery; University of Western Australia.

HUGH RAMSAY
New South Wales, Victorian, South Australian, Queensland, Western Australian and Tasmanian State galleries; Geelong, Bendigo and Castlemaine galleries.

TOM ROBERTS
New South Wales (31 works), Victorian, South Australian, Queensland, Western Australian and Tasmanian State galleries; Bendigo, Geelong, Ballarat and Castlemaine galleries; National Collection, Canberra.

ARTHUR STREETON
New South Wales, Victorian, South Australian, Queensland and Western Australian State galleries; Bendigo, Geelong, Newcastle, Ballarat, Mildura, Shepparton and Castlemaine galleries; Australian National War Memorial (56 works), Canberra.

WILLIAM STRUTT
New South Wales, South Australian and Tasmanian State galleries; Ballarat gallery; Mitchell Library, Sydney; National Library, Canberra; State Library and Parliamentary Library, Melbourne.

WALTER WITHERS
New South Wales, Victorian, South Australian, Queensland, Western Australian and Tasmanian State galleries; Bendigo, Geelong, Ballarat and Castlemaine galleries; University of Western Australia.

Index

Arthur Streeton
Golden summer (1889)
Oil on panel 81.2 x 152.4
Private collection